Follow Me Around™
United Kingdom

By Wiley Blevins

SCHOLASTIC

Content Consultant: Caleb Richardson, PhD, Assistant Professor,
Department of History, University of New Mexico, Albuquerque, New Mexico

Library of Congress Cataloging-in-Publication Data
Names: Blevins, Wiley, author. Title: United Kingdom / by Wiley Blevins.
Description: New York, NY : Children's Press, 2018. | Series: Follow me around | Includes bibliographical references and index.
Identifiers: LCCN 2017030754 | ISBN 9780531234570 (library binding) | ISBN 9780531243695 (pbk.)
Subjects: LCSH: Great Britain—Juvenile literature. | Great   Britain—Description and travel—Juvenile literature.
Classification: LCC DA27.5 .B585 2018 | DDC 941—dc23
LC record available at https://lccn.loc.gov/2017030754

Design: Judith Christ Lafond & Anna Tunick Tabachnik
Text: Wiley Blevins
© 2018 Scholastic Inc.

All rights reserved. Published in 2018 by Children's Press, an imprint of Scholastic Inc.
Printed in North Mankato, MN, USA 113
SCHOLASTIC, CHILDREN'S PRESS, and associated logos are trademarks and/or registered trademarks of Scholastic Inc.
Scholastic Inc., 557 Broadway, New York, NY 10012

1 2 3 4 5 6 7 8 9 10 R 27 26 25 24 23 22 21 20 19 18

Photos ©: cover background: Jon Arnold Images Ltd/Alamy Images; cover child: Nick David/Getty Images; back cover: Nick David/Getty Images; 1: Nick David/Getty Images; 3: Pushkin/Shutterstock; 4 left: Nick David/Getty Images; 6: Ron Ellis/Shutterstock; 7 left: mubus7/Shutterstock; 7 right: Andy Sutton/Alamy Images; 8 left: monkeybusinessimages/iStockphoto; 8 center right: martinrlee/iStockphoto; 8 bottom right: Ryzhkov Photography/Shutterstock; 8 top right: Lisovskaya/iStockphoto; 9 center: stockcreations/Shutterstock; 9 left: ArtCookStudio/iStockphoto; 9 right: ALLEKO/iStockphoto; 10: Roger Bamber/Alamy Images; 11: Keith Morris/Media Bakery; 12 right: doddis77/Shutterstock; 12 left: Pushkin/Shutterstock; 12-13 background: Vadim Yerofeyev/Dreamstime; 13 top: Stocklifemax/Shutterstock; 13 bottom: Pushkin/Shutterstock; 14 top left: YipunJJ/Shutterstock; 14 top right: Luciano Mortula-LGM/Shutterstock; 14 bottom: QQ7/iStockphoto; 15 left: cdbrphotography/iStockphoto; 15 right: Tim Moore/Alamy Images; 16 left: Roll6/iStockphoto; 16 top right: Marbury/iStockphoto; 16 bottom right: Paul Faith-PA Images/Getty Images; 17 top left: Jason Hawkes/Getty Images; 17 right: Robert Birkby/AWL Images; 17 bottom left: Keystone/Getty Images; 18 top: Lebrecht Music and Arts Photo Library/Alamy Images; 18 bottom left: Lanmas/Alamy Images; 18 bottom right: lightphoto/iStockphoto; 19 left: Portrait of William the Conqueror (1027-87), English School, (16th century)/Private Collection/Photo © Philip Mould Ltd, London/Bridgeman Art Library; 19 center: Central Press/Getty Images; 19 right: Chris Jackson/Getty Images; 20 right: Robbie Jack/Getty Images; 20 left: Getty Images; 21 right: Iain Masterton/Getty Images; 21 left: Slavko Sereda/Shutterstock; 22: Anwar Hussein/Getty Images; 23 top left: AFP/Getty Images; 23 center left top: Jeff J Mitchell/Getty Images; 23 center left bottom: SolStock/Getty Images; 23 center right: SolStock/iStockphoto; 23 top right: Eduardo Rocha/Shutterstock; 24 left: Paul Ellis/Getty Images; 24 top right: PeopleImages/Getty Images; 24 bottom right: Diarmid Courreges/Getty Images; 25 left: Gregory Shamus/Getty Images; 25 right: Alan Edwards/Alamy Images; 26 right: Jane McIlroy/Shutterstock; 26 left: Jaroslaw Kilian/Shutterstock; 27 top left: CreativeMedia.org.uk/Shutterstock; 27 bottom: MentalArt/iStockphoto; 27 top right: skynesher/iStockphoto; 28 A: Vittorio Caramazza/Shutterstock; 28 C: JustinBlackStock/iStockphoto; 28 D: Gannet77/iStockphoto; 28 E: BasPhoto/Shutterstock; 28 F: Jeff Gilbert/Alamy Images; 28 G: VisitBritain/Jason Hawkes/Getty Images; 28 B: jcarillet/iStockphoto; 29: Andrey Lobachev/Shutterstock; 30 top right: Ismailciydem/iStockphoto; 30 top left: MargaretClavell/iStockphoto; 30 bottom: Nick David/Getty Images.
Maps by Jim McMahon.

Table of Contents

Where in the World Is the United Kingdom? 4

Home Sweet Home.. 6

Let's Eat!.. 8

Off to School... 10

The Legend of King Arthur 12

Touring the United Kingdom 14

Our Fascinating History 18

It Came From the United Kingdom 20

Celebrate! 22

Time to Play.. 24

You Won't Believe This!.................................. 26

Guessing Game!..28

Preparing for Your Visit 29

The United States Compared to the United Kingdom... 30

Glossary 31

Index.. 32

United Kingdom

USA

Where in the World Is the United Kingdom?

Hello! Good day to you from the United Kingdom! I'm Isla, your tour guide. My name means "island," and comes from Scottish Gaelic, a language from Scotland. I hope that someday you'll visit my beautiful island country.

The United Kingdom is located in northwestern Europe. It is made up of four separate regions: England, Scotland, Wales, and Northern Ireland. England, Scotland, and Wales are all located on the island of Great Britain. Northern Ireland is located on the nearby island of Ireland. It shares the island with the Republic of Ireland, a separate country.

Each of the four regions in the United Kingdom has its own capital. All the different parts of my country offer many interesting things to see and do. Let me show you around!

Fast Facts:

- **The United Kingdom covers 93,628 square miles (242,495 square kilometers).**

- **The United Kingdom is referred to as the U.K.**

- **The Severn and the Thames are the longest rivers in the U.K.**

- **The U.K. also includes thousands of nearby tiny islands. These include the Orkney Islands, the Shetland Islands, the Isle of Wight, and others.**

- **The U.K. enjoys four seasons: spring, summer, fall, and winter. Temperatures are seldom extremely hot or cold, but most places do get a lot of rain!**

ATLANTIC OCEAN

North Sea

NORWAY

Scotland

UNITED KINGDOM

DENMARK

Northern Ireland

Manchester

IRELAND

England

NETHERLANDS

Wales

London

River Thames

BELGIUM

GERMANY

Celtic Sea

English Channel

LUX.

FRANCE

SWITZ.

Bay of Biscay

ITALY

Home Sweet Home

I am from London, England. I live with my parents in a row house. It is also known as a terraced house. All the houses on my block look alike. Houses like mine have been around for hundreds of years in big cities. We have a small yard in the back where my *mum* (mother) grows flowers. My big brother lives in a nearby *flat*, which is what you call an apartment in the United States.

Every Saturday, I go with my mum to an open market. There, we buy fruits and vegetables. Sometimes I can even find a toy or a T-shirt that I like. When I'm not helping my mum, I like to watch the *telly* (TV) or play video games.

Cottage

Villages were built around the town church or manor house, the most important places in the town.

Travel outside my city and you'll see a lot of country homes. These charming cottages are often surrounded by big gardens filled with colorful flowers. Many of the cottages are hundreds of years old. Some are made of local stones and come in a variety of colors. Others are made of wood with **thatched** roofs.

You'll also drive through small villages. These villages first popped up around 1,500 years ago. They are organized around a village square. There, you'll usually find a big cathedral, which is a large church, or a **manor house**. Walking through some of these villages is like stepping back in time. You'll love it!

Many families like to share dinner together.

Curry

Fish and chips

Let's Eat!

The food in the United Kingdom is as diverse as its people and history. Our breakfasts are similar to those in the United States—cereal, eggs, toast, and meat. For lunch, we usually have a quick sandwich. Dinner is our main meal. My family loves Indian food with its yummy curry sauces. When people from India moved to the U.K. beginning in the 1800s, they brought lots of curry recipes.

The most popular traditional dish here is probably fish and chips. The fish is battered and fried. It is so good! The chips are what you call french fries. Some people eat this dish with gravy, mushy peas, or curry sauce. There's also our famous shepherd's pie. No, it's not a dessert. It's made with ground beef and mashed potatoes.

Shepherd's pie

Black pudding

Haggis

Scones with jam

Tea

If you're feeling adventurous, try black pudding. This dish is made from pig's blood. It's tastier than it sounds. There's also haggis, a Scottish specialty. It's like a sausage made from chopped sheep's heart, lungs, and liver mixed with oatmeal, onions, and spices. Yum, though not for everyone!

No day is complete without afternoon tea. Have it with a scone, and spread on some jam and clotted cream. Clotted cream is a thick cream similar to butter. Teatime began in the mid-1800s, when a duchess complained of a "sinking" feeling in the afternoon. She began asking for tea and a light snack to regain energy. Soon, she started inviting friends. The tradition caught on.

Tea Etiquette

Remember these afternoon tea tips!

- **Don't stir** your tea in a circular motion with a spoon.

- **Don't clink** the spoon against the cup. (It's hard not to!)

- Put the spoon on the **saucer** behind the cup. It should be to the right of the handle.

- **Don't loop** your fingers through the cup handle.

- Pour in the milk **after** pouring in the tea.

- Sip your tea **quietly**. Never slurp!

Boarding school dorm room

Off to School

In the U.K., most kids go to school from ages 5 to 18. Some students finish at age 16 and go to a trade school. There, they study for a specific job. Others stay in school and prepare for college. We call each grade a year. We start at year 1, then go to year 2, and so on. Our year 1 would be called kindergarten in the United States. Year 2 here is your first grade.

Some students live at boarding schools. Most of these schools are "public." What we call "public" schools are the opposite of public schools in the United States. Here, students pay a fee to attend a public school, but the school is open to everyone no matter where they live. We also sometimes call them independent schools.

A sign in Wales written in Welsh and English

Ysgol
School

One of the first things we learn in school is how to read and write in English. It is our official language. We use the Roman alphabet with its 26 letters, just like you do in the United States. However, some of the words we use are spelled differently here. Others are completely different words.

Some areas of the U.K. have their own languages, too. In Wales, many people learn Welsh. Scottish Gaelic is spoken in Scotland, and Irish Gaelic in Northern Ireland. People in Cornwall, in southern England, may learn Cornish.

How Do You Say It?

Before you visit, learn some of the differences between U.K. English and U.S. English.

United Kingdom	United States
biscuit	cookie
lorries	trucks
loo	bathroom
jumper	sweater
trainers	sneakers
crisps	potato chips
lift	elevator
bangers	sausages
bin	trash
telly	TV
bap, batch, cob, barm, muffin, bridie, rowie, stottie, and oggie	bread roll

The Legend of King Arthur

In school, we read a lot of legends about kings, dragons, and castles from long ago. One of my favorites is the legend of King Arthur and the sword in the stone.

Long ago, there lived a boy named Arthur. He was the son of the king of England, but he didn't know that. When he was a baby, Arthur was given to a family at a nearby castle in secret. Only Merlin, a wise wizard, knew who Arthur was.

Soon after Arthur's birth, the king died. Most people didn't know about Arthur, the rightful next king, so the country fell into chaos. Dukes and lords fought over who would rule England. To help bring peace, they asked Merlin to choose a leader and save the kingdom.

Merlin came up with a clever plan. He placed a magical sword in a stone. On the sword's blade was written, "Whoever pulls out this sword from this stone is the rightful King of

England." Many important people pulled and tugged at the sword with all their might, but all failed.

Meanwhile, Arthur was growing up. He was not treated well at the castle where he lived, and he felt out of place. But Merlin made sure the boy was safe. He taught Arthur many things. The most important lesson was that knowledge is greater than force. Arthur learned that a wise ruler uses his head before his fists. Arthur and Merlin grew to be friends.

Sixteen years went by, and England still had not found a king. One day, when a large crowd had gathered around the sword and the stone, Merlin led young Arthur to it. No one believed this teenage boy could be the next king. But Arthur was the king's son. Arthur carefully grabbed the sword's handle and slowly slid it out of the stone. The crowd erupted in cheers. "Long live our new king. Long live King Arthur!"

Changing the Guard

Big Ben

Touring the United Kingdom

London: Capital City

Welcome to my city, London. It's the capital of the United Kingdom. It is also the capital of England. London sits on the winding River Thames. When you visit, you'll want to go first to Buckingham Palace. That's one of the queen's homes. Make sure you don't miss the Changing the Guard ceremony out front. Then head over to Big Ben. It's the giant, loud bell that rings in the most famous clock in the world. On your way there, you can stop at Westminster Abbey. Many kings, queens, and famous people are buried in this old church.

A short walk away is a new landmark—the London Eye. It's a giant Ferris wheel. Hop on and get a bird's-eye view of my city.

London Eye

Thames

Hyde Park

Catch a ride on the Tube and speed all over London. The Tube is our underground railway, or subway. It was the first subway ever built in the world. Make sure you stop at Hyde Park if it's a sunny day. You can boat or swim in the lake, or ride horses. You can also take a stroll through Kensington Gardens, which is connected to the park. If you like a mystery, head over to the Sherlock Holmes Museum to learn about our most popular detective. Another must-see spot is the Tower of London. It was once a home for royalty and a famous prison. Today, it houses the Crown Jewels—the gems that have been worn by our kings and queens. The place is filled with ravens. These black birds can be a bit spooky. Legend has it that if these ravens leave the Tower of London, then the entire kingdom will fall. So be nice to them!

Edinburgh Castle

Wild horses at the Cardiff coast

Ulster Museum

Other Capitals: Edinburgh, Cardiff, and Belfast

More than 80 percent of people in the U.K. live in cities and towns. After you leave London, visit the capitals of the other regions for a taste of city life across the country. Edinburgh is the capital of Scotland. Edinburgh Castle here has plenty of nooks and crannies to explore. After that, take the fright-filled Cadies and Witchery Tour through the old part of the city.

Cardiff, on the coast, is the capital of Wales. See great castles and cathedrals in this city. You can also step back in time at the Saint Fagan's National Museum of History. It's an outdoor museum that is a lot of fun!

You can take a boat to Belfast, the capital of Northern Ireland. Go to Cave Hill to hike, picnic, and see a range of ancient sites. The Ulster Museum is also terrific. It is chock-full of dinosaurs and mummies.

Stonehenge

Loch Ness

This photo was once believed to show the Loch Ness monster. Most people now agree it is fake.

Stonehenge and Loch Ness

As you travel through the winding roads and historic villages outside our cities, there are two stops you must make. One is Stonehenge. People first started building this prehistoric stone **monument** in about 3000 BCE. No one knows how it was built or why. Some people think it's a calendar connected to the movements of the sun. There are other ancient sites nearby worth visiting too.

The other stop you should make is in Scotland. There, visit Loch Ness. It's a big loch, or lake. It is said to be home to the famous Loch Ness monster. Tourists flood this lake to catch a glimpse of "Nessie." Take your camera. Maybe you'll be the first person in years to spot this water creature!

Our Fascinating History

Our country has a long history filled with kings, queens, and battles. The Celts were one of the first groups to settle here thousands of years ago. The Romans invaded in about 55 BCE. The Celtic queen Boudicca is famous for fighting the Romans, though she was defeated. The Romans built many roads, walls, and cities. Some of these structures still exist today. In the 400s, Anglo-Saxons from Europe replaced the Romans. They created many small kingdoms.

Queen Boudicca

Timeline: The United Kingdom History

Romans on Britain's shores

Anglo-Saxon helmet

2000 BCE

Celts
Groups from Europe settle on the island that is now Great Britain.

55 BCE

Romans
Romans invade parts of the island and claim it for the Roman **Empire**.

400s CE

Anglo-Saxons
Germanic tribes from Europe settle parts of the island. Many modern English words come from Anglo-Saxon.

Then in 1066, Normans from what is now France defeated the Anglo-Saxons. William the Conqueror took power. Since then, we have had a series of kings and queens.

Starting in the late 1500s, the U.K. took over lands all around the globe. Many of these countries eventually regained independence. But some, such as Australia and Canada, are still tied together in a **Commonwealth**. Today, our queen has very little power. We are a **democracy** with an elected prime minister and parliament, much like the U.S. president and Congress.

William the Conqueror

1066

William the Conqueror
The Norman Conquest begins a long line of English kings and queens.

BRITAIN DECLARES WAR
EXPRESS
SPECIAL LATE NEWS

1500s–1900s

British Empire
British troops take over lands all over the world to create the largest empire the world has ever seen.

1914–1918, 1939–1945

World Wars
The U.K. takes part in World War I and World War II. Its allies include the United States.

Queen Elizabeth II

1952–today

Queen Elizabeth II
Our current queen has been ruling for more than 60 years. She is the longest serving ruler in U.K. history.

It Came From the United Kingdom

William Shakespeare lived in the late 1500s and early 1600s and wrote plays. Some of his most famous ones are *Romeo and Juliet, Hamlet, Macbeth,* and *Much Ado About Nothing.* His plays introduced more than 1,700 new words into the English language. *Generous, birthplace, lonely, gossip, swagger,* and *zany* are just a few examples.

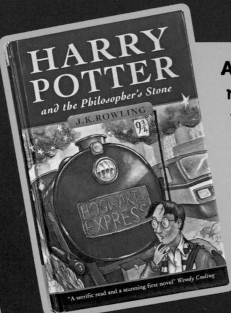

A lot of amazing books you've heard about, read, or will read come from the U.K. These include *A Christmas Carol; Frankenstein; Alice's Adventures in Wonderland; Robinson Crusoe; Charlie and the Chocolate Factory; The Lion, the Witch, and the Wardrobe;* and, of course, the Harry Potter books. You should read them all!

Scotland is famous for its bagpipes and kilts. Bagpipes are a musical instrument. They make a very distinct sound. Kilts are like skirts and are worn by both women and men. They come in many different patterns. Each family group, or clan, has its own special pattern. Some of the best-known clans are MacLeod, Mackay, MacDonald, Mackenzie, Campbell, Douglas, Stuart, Gordon, Fraser, and Sinclair.

Northern Ireland is known for the shamrock, which is a three-leaf clover. Keep an eye out for a four-leaf clover, too. These are rare—and lucky! The land is also known for its leprechauns. These tiny fairies are rumored to hide in a pot of gold. Where is the pot? At the end of a rainbow, of course!

Trooping the Colour

Celebrate!

Everyone loves a holiday, and we have some fun ones in the U.K. My favorite is Trooping the Colour, which occurs here in London in June. It includes the queen's official birthday parade. Red-coated soldiers show off their colorful flags, and the queen rides in a beautiful horse-drawn carriage. Then she and her family stand on the balcony of Buckingham Palace. Royal Air Force planes fly past, leaving behind red, white, and blue streams of color. Amazing!

Other Fun Celebrations

March

August

November 5

December

St. Patrick's Day

This day celebrates the island of Ireland's patron saint. There are big celebrations in Northern Ireland and in the rest of the U.K.

Edinburgh Military Tattoo

Enjoy the sounds of bagpipers and drummers as military groups across the U.K. and the world perform.

Bonfire Night

Also known as Guy Fawkes Day, bonfires and fireworks help remember the day in our history that a man named Guy Fawkes failed to burn down the building where Parliament meets.

Christmas

Here, this holiday lasts 12 days, from December 25 to January 5. Father Christmas, presents, and mince (chopped meat) pies are all traditions.

Make Leprechaun Doughnuts

Create these treats as a trap for the mythical leprechaun. The tiny doughnuts are just the right size for one of these tiny fairies!

Ingredients: 1/2 cup sugar; 1/2 cup water; small round cereal pieces (such as Cheerios); toppings

Directions:

Ask an adult to help!

1 **Combine** the sugar and water in a pot. **Boil** the water until the sugar dissolves. This creates sugar water.

2 **Dip** a piece of cereal in the sugar water.

3 **Roll** the cereal in your topping (icing, powdered sugar, etc.).

4 **Repeat** steps 2 and 3 until you have several tiny doughnuts.

To construct a trap to catch a leprechaun, stack 2 to 3 regular-sized doughnuts. Pour the tiny leprechaun doughnuts inside the hole. When the leprechaun hops on to munch away, he'll fall in. Gotcha!

Soccer

Cricket

Rugby

Time to Play

Kids in the U.K. love their football. This is what you call soccer in the United States. It is our most popular sport, and many boys and girls play it. Our best-known teams have fans all over the world. These include Chelsea, Manchester United, and Liverpool. Their players are superstars to us.

Our national sport, however, is cricket. It's a bat-and-ball game that is a little like baseball. Two teams of 11 play on a grassy field. Spectators watch and picnic nearby. Another common sport is rugby. It's similar to American football, but players don't wear helmets or protective pads! This sport began in the U.K.

Golf

Netball

Two other sports connected to the U.K. are tennis and golf. Tennis started as a game for kings. Each year at our famous Wimbledon tennis courts, players from all over the world compete.

Modern-day golf began in Scotland. It is more than 500 years old. In the 1500s, Mary, the queen of Scotland, liked to play this game. Young people training for the military, called cadets, carried her golf clubs for her. That's why people who carry golf clubs today are called caddies.

My friends and I also like dancing, martial arts, skateboarding, cycling, and netball. I am captain of my netball team at school. This sport is a lot like basketball. One big difference is that each player can only move around in a certain part of the court. Also, we can only hold on to the ball for three seconds. You have to act fast in this sport!

You Won't Believe This!

Unlike in the United States, we drive on the left side of the road. The driver sits on the right side of the car. This started during the days of horse-drawn carriages. Carriage drivers kept swords with them in case they needed to defend themselves. Because most people are right-handed, it is easiest to fight someone located to their right. Driving on the left placed any drivers traveling the opposite way on the carriage's right side.

Some places here have long names. I mean really long! The longest is the Welsh town of Llanfairpwllgwyngyllgogerychwyrndrobwll-llantysiliogogogoch. Its name means "The Church of Mary in the hollow of the white hazel near the fierce whirlpool and the Church of Tysilio by the red cave."

The Metropolitan Police Act of 1839 made it illegal for kids to slide on ice or snow, fly a kite, set off fireworks, ring a doorbell without permission, or tease a bear. These laws are still in place today. What do you think about that?

Our roads have some interesting names. You might find yourself wandering on Ha-Ha Road in Greenwich or Silly Lane in Lancaster. But try not to giggle!

The sandwich was invented by the Earl of Sandwich. He was playing cards and didn't want to stop, but he needed a snack. He asked his servants to put some meat between two pieces of bread. This made the meal easy to pick up and eat—and the earl never had to leave the card table!

Guessing Game!

Here are some other great sites around the United Kingdom. If you have time, try to see them all!

1. Windsor Castle
2. White Cliffs of Dover
3. Roman Baths
4. Giant's Causeway
5. Oxford University
6. Hadrian's Wall
7. Brighton Palace Pier

A

You're sure to have fun at this seaside amusement park. It is built on a platform called a pier that juts out into the sea.

This castle is one of the official homes of the queen.

E

F

Stroll around the campus of England's oldest university.

B

The result of volcanic activity, this is one of the great natural wonders of the U.K. According to legend, a giant built it.

These famous white cliffs welcome travelers crossing the English Channel.

G

D

This protective wall dating back to 122 CE was built by the Roman emperor Hadrian. It marked the northern limit of the Roman Empire at the time.

C

Take a dip in these open-air baths found in Bath, a city that the Romans built long ago.

28

Preparing for Your Visit

By now, you should be ready to hop on a plane to the United Kingdom. Here are some tips to prepare for your trip.

1 Before you come to the U.K., exchange your money. Our money is called pound sterling, or "pound" for short. You'll need it to buy fun **souvenirs**. It takes 100 pence, or pennies, to make one pound. The queen's picture is on our money, and it has been updated many times. If you take a close look, you can see how she's changed over time.

2 If you have an emergency while you're traveling, just dial 999. You can also ask a bobby, or police officer, for help. You might also spot a police constable. You'll know a constable by the traditional black hat he or she wears.

3 There are many British accents. If you go to the east, you might hear *help* pronounced "'elp." People there tend to drop the h from words. In the southeast, many people drop the r at the end of words. *Forever* becomes "forevuh." And in my city, London, some people speak Cockney. It's **slang** that uses rhymes. For example, *head* might be replaced with *crust*, as in "crust of bread." So you might hear someone say, "Use your crust." That means, "Use your head!"

4 Bring an adapter for your electronics. This is a special plug that allows your electronics to fit into the outlet. Otherwise you won't be able to charge your phone or tablet. Not good!

The United States Compared the to United Kingdom

Official Name	United States of America (USA)	The United Kingdom of Great Britain and Northern Ireland (U.K.)
Official Language	No official language, though English is most commonly used	English
Population	325 million	65 million
Flag		Known as the Union Jack
Money	Dollar	Pound sterling (pound)
Location	North America	Northwestern Europe
Highest Point	Denali (Mount McKinley)	Ben Nevis (Scotland)
Lowest Point	Death Valley	Holme Fen (England)
Size	World's third-largest country	About 1/3 the size of Texas
National Anthem	"The Star-Spangled Banner"	"God Save the Queen"

So now you know some important and fascinating things about my country, the United Kingdom. I hope to see you someday exploring one of our historic capital cities, riding the Tube through London, or sightseeing at Stonehenge. Until then . . . *cheers*! Good-bye.

Glossary

commonwealth
(KAH-muhn-welth)
a group of countries that includes the U.K. and many countries that were once part of the British Empire; the British queen is the commonwealth's symbolic ruler

democracy
(dih-MAH-kruh-see)
a form of government in which the people choose their leaders in elections

empire
(EM-pire)
a group of countries or states that have the same ruler

manor house
(MAN-ur HOUS)
the traditional home of the lord, or person who controlled an area of land in the 13th through 15th centuries

monument
(MAHN-yuh-muhnt)
an important statue, building, or other structure

slang
(SLANG)
colorful or lively words and phrases used in ordinary conversation but not in formal speech or writing

souvenirs
(soo-vuh-NEERZ)
objects that you keep to remind you of a place, person, or something that happened

thatched
(THACHT)
made of dried plants, such as straw or reeds

Index

cities, 6, 14–15, 16, 18, 28, 29
food, 6, 8–9, 27
history, 18–19, 20, 28
holidays, 22–23

homes, 6–7, 14, 15
land, 4–5, 19
languages, 4, 11, 20, 29, 30
legends, 12–13, 15, 17

money, 29, 30
regions, 4, 16
roads, 18, 26, 27
school, 10–11, 12, 25
sports, 24–25

Facts for Now

Visit this Scholastic website for more information on the United Kingdom and to download the Teaching Guide for this series:

www.factsfornow.scholastic.com   Enter the keywords **United Kingdom**

About the Author

Wiley Blevins lives and works in New York City. His greatest love is traveling, and he has been to the United Kingdom many times. He has written several books for children, including the Ick and Crud series and the Scary Tales Retold series.